In *Back Cut,* Ann Spiers accomplishes the rare feat of weaving lyrical poems into a compelling narrative. Set in the mid-twentieth century, two characters—"Husband" and "Wife"—struggle to support themselves in the depleted landscape of the Olympic Coast after the great forests have been cut down and the clam beds ravaged for commerce. In poems as spare and language as angular as the couple themselves, the reader is taken on a journey of pain and beauty as the man and woman drag the long nets, light damp wood in iron stoves, and reflect on their love, their neighbors, and their remote, haggard world. Spiers gives us that world back again--bears, salmon, flotsam cabins, even a wild man--in sea-swept poems of compelling beauty and depth. — Sharon Cumberland, author of *Peculiar Honors* and *Strange with Age*; two-time winner, First Prize for Poetry, Pacific Northwest Writers Association

As the title suggests, the poems in Ann Spiers' latest collection *Back Cut* come at their subject indirectly, tell their truth slant. Through a powerful series of persona poems, Spiers recreates the not-so-distant era, after the tall trees had fallen, of the men and women who subsist on the outer edge of the Washington coast. Here, husband and wife tell their stories in words as earthy as the land and as salty as the sea where they eke out a living. As wildness still shines through the clear cuts, tenderness glints in the spaces of what's not said. Spiers describes the collection as a love story, and love story it is, not just between husband and wife, but between humans and the land that sustains them. Kudos to Spiers, who renders it all so vividly we can taste each briny clam, claim our complex Northwest history.
— Holly J. Hughes, author of *Hold Fast*; winner of the American Book Award

Back Cut

Back Cut

Ann Spiers

Black Heron Press
Post Office Box 614
Anacortes, Washington 98221
www.blackheronpress.com

Some of the poems in *Back Cut* appeared in the following publications: *A Sense of Place: The Washington State Geospatial Poetry Anthology*; *Fire on Her Tongue: Anthology of Contemporary Women's Poetry*; *Raven Chronicles*; *Soundings Review*; *Fiberarts*; *About Place Journal*. Other poems appeared in these chapbooks: *What Rain Does* (Egress Studio), *Bunker Trail* (Finishing Line Press). Some poems appeared in slightly different forms and under different titles. *Back Cut*'s characters originated in the poet's imagination, and its settings are an amalgamation of places. Any resemblance to persons living or dead is entirely coincidental.

ISBN: 978-1-936364-38-1

Black Heron Press
Post Office Box 614
Anacortes, Washington 98221
www.blackheronpress.com

To David Frank, my true love

Contents

Introduction

In felling a tree, the initial deep undercut is wedge shaped. This cut determines the direction of fall. Opposite and higher than the initial cut is the back cut, the first of the felling cuts. The labor varies with tree, axe or saw, and with the crew's strength and smarts.

These poems detail the ocean edge of Washington State immediately after World War II and after the forest's big cut and last commercial razor clam digs. In that decade, folks eked out a living on the dwindling supply of these natural resources.

This is a love story.

Wife—
Methuselah's Beard

i

Old Man Sampson straightens
    his flannel shirt faded to grey
    cigarette behind his ear
    face stubble long as it will get
he stands in the bright color
of cedar shakes freshly split
day in and day out

he waves his arm
a generous invite
    to go at it ourselves
split our own shakes
or leave some coins
    nickel per piece
honor system

I run a U-Shake he jokes
the old coot shows off
    his froe cleaves the wood
    he twists its haft
iron splitting shakes
    from the bolt's fresh edge.

ii

My husband picks up the tools
tries a hit and another
    the split not clean
    its length short
    of the 24 inches allowing
    ten inches to the weather

Sampson says *It's the drinking*
    you gotta give it up

my love answers *Not on your life*
stuffs a few dollars
    into the coffee can atop a stump
he shoulders
his bundles of shakes
    plenty to roof half a shed.

iii

Yes my love
no one does as much weight
 lift and set down
moving cedar dugouts up beach
 pry and push
his long-handled peavey
 wrangling logs into place

Saint Christopher himself
 carrying over streams
 fast and frothy
white ladies
 fat with larded pies
and Indian women
 plump with fry bread
 dipped in seal oil
everybody laughing

my drunken man
 flexing
 noise
 showoff.

iv

We buck down the road
I say *Old Man Sampson knows*
    what he is about
I hang my arm out the window
    my fingers combing
    the dismal light
we roll through woods
hung with Methuselah's Beard
a lichen
so proficient
    it eats the air
I say *I don't mind being here*
the smell of cedar
    holding me

my love downshifts
    the high pitch of metal on metal
    brakes smoking
indecent thoughts rise in me
about Old Man Sampson undressed
he all white under his stiff clothes
except for his face and hands
    sun leathered and work cut
    rough as a scabby apple

I pull my hand in
from the rushing air
it finds its mate as I slide
them between my legs
my desire taking me
   somewhere else.

Husband—
Clam Gun

i
Midnight
I button her slicker
my fingers arguing
with the last metal hook
    winter low tide a pulse
    out there in the pitch
razor clam holes
pock the beach
like a disease

I drag the long-nosed net
behind me its harness
    a soft cross
    strapped across my chest
I work bent forward
pushing into the sand
the tube of my clam gun
    like a biscuit cutter
    pulling up pucks of beach
I fist the clams
from the tide's gullet

she holds the lantern high
between the surf and me
she places her hand
   on my shoulder
the seventh wave
   ramps in
   floods the beach
we are jetsam
   anchored lightly
the outrush sucks
sand from underfoot
   unbalancing us
the entire sea returns
to fill our boots.

ii
I say *We're good*
   at what we do
money in my pocket
even if the cannery man
lightens my clams' weight
   his gnarly thumb lifting
   the scale's backside

past 2 a.m. the tavern closed
we take the beach home
Talk to me I say
she says *I can't hear myself*
   over the ocean

behind the firs
dawn rising
I say *Think of the coffee*
and cash for real cream

she says *It's the tide coming in*
she says *I hear the tide coming in*
she says *Hurry.*

iii

She pulls
    her warmed hands
    from under the pillow
she touches her fingertips to her nose
    the scent brine and clam

my fingers stink with work
my hands soft with seawater
    still swollen with cold
sun flooding our cabin
my hands don't shake
    as I unbutton her

I am on my knees
lighting the fire
matchbox emptying
    stick after stick
striking finally
on the underbelly
of a wet rock.

Wife—
A Lot of Man

i
In Seattle after the war
he was small unfixed
    cigarette hanging
      from his dry bottom lip
a shadow in our boarding house
just mustered out of the 106th Infantry
barbed wire scars fresh on his hands
and drunk on more than victory

    out here
he fills our cabin
he built with flotsam
    boards reeking of brine
and with rusted nails
    pulled from sheds
    collapsed

    out here
he is a gathering storm
his voice cracks
    reverbs off sea cliffs
his stories filter through a crowd
    lightning sieving through fir
his heat melts the room

some women hold sour memories
let me Lord keep
the generous moments
my true love standing
    when women enter the room
he first with a cup of boiled coffee
    proffered from his two hands
    warming our pilfered crockery
his hands shaking with use.

ii
I dig late potatoes
    purples scabby small
    a cross of Ozette Blues
    and some orphan
    up Dickey River
roots spread out and out
bumped with spuds

potatoes all winter
just the size to soften
at the first boil no need
    for the water to giggle
    for an hour
then unwatched
    boil over
    burnt starch
    marking the woodstove

good ground is hard to find
all this rain
    heavy in the clouds
hangs mid air
condenses on my cheeks

into the muck
I plant potatoes
    eyes blind
    skin wrinkled.

Husband—
Putting Up For Winter

The glut
we net smelt out
of the wave's long running
eagles snag silver scattering
crazy

salmon
so plentiful
their splishes racket up
stream   bear smell hot at every
trail turn

so thick
huckleberry
milked from the stem plunk plunk
in our buckets   fresh scat purple
with fruit

so much
we cannot stop
bigger loads just one more
woodstove glowing into the night
horse clams

dozens
jarred up erect
apple slices strung on
make-do rigging across the room
zigzag

so much
heat steam and smoke
days nights fill with doing
one by one   too much   oh thank god
hunger.

Wife—
Gift

i
I did hear my baby cry
I hear that sound tonight
    from the holly thicket
    red berries shiny prickles
an owlet mews
    for its parents to bring
    mice and more mice
I tell my love this twice.

ii
He finds it on the beach
green army man
toy soldier with helmet
    heavy boots
    rifle across his chest

he slows to let me
catch up
    him leaning
    into the wind

he says
Dime store soldier
100 for 50 cents
sea roughed him up
and now no face

he kicks
at the beached drift
he says
Look for
his brothers in arms

I say *Big ocean.*

iii

He says
We had faces
bayonets sharpened
boots spit shined

he says
We were the best
    the clutch of us
taking a town
        empty
        except for a few crazies
        us humping through
cafes cleaned of food
except a coffee cup
        mid table surviving
        dried brown on the bottom
we'd pour canteen water into it
rub around with our fingers
get a slug or two of real joe

this time he doesn't say
We were grunts fodder

I pocket the green soldier
eyes nose mouth
smoothed
for that baby
without a face yet.

iv

Working today's clearcut
I lop boughs at thirty inches
    stacking flat sprays
    gathering cedar and fir
    acres of fallen green and pitch
long dark by four

he is beside me
    binding hauling the bundles
he knows Christmas
by the weight of these loads
    ten twenty thirty pounds.

v

The owlet chafes for food
parents returning again
must be male
to cry ragged like that

the greens buyer
weighs our load
    dollars for our pounds
    of baled Christmas

I say
We can buy a gift
for our someday Alexander
an army of marching men.

Husband—
Copalis Crossing

i
The banana bread is done
when she inserts a straw
     into its risen dome
and the gesture brings back
     all the times
she yanked the straw
     out of the kitchen broom
punctured the crust
and loved the clean pullout
     me and the warm bread
     gone.

ii

At the table
I tug
a fist full of seeds
out of the pumpkin

she stands
   in the open door
watches the rain
   fill the ditches
   and now run
   the road's long ruts
this is how
autumn slips away
and how again the rain
   keeps us inside
   alone.

iii

I say
something about the moon
    rounding for winter
I watch her posed there
    looking into the night
    ready to close the door

right then
how her skin glows
makes me think
    of light flowing off
    the great heron's wings
I open my mouth
the image that lifted
    me closer to her
    gone.

iv
Connor Creek
is bank to bank
and by dark noon
its water runs
    into the woods
    pushing leaf fall
    carrying silt

treefrogs croak

she closes the door

the woodstove
    tick ticks
joints expanding
metal swelling

heat
the curtain stirs
its belly stuck
to the sweating
window.

v
She says
I saw jellyfish

her remembering jellyfish
lulled to shore where waves lap
    sharply over cobbles

she cups her hands under one
a colorless moon
    its yellow gonads
    complicate its clear bell
creature slipping through her fingers
    back into the sea

Jellyfish
I say
Everything in your hand
is like that
    slippery
    gone.

Wife—
Summer Lady

i
There she is
I never saw her before
she must be summer people
    her in her gray clothes
    skirt and shirt not tucked in
    and clogs odd choice
    for uneven ground
but she's up and socks dry
she smells of turpentine
    and almond-scented lotion

he knows what she wants
he points to back there
    where after we strip the flesh
he throws fish heads deer guts
    tough chicken bits
    old clams gaping with stink.

ii

Before us before anyone
the goat lady squatted here
    alone at the beach edge
    no man and no women
    no one to visit
just goats crowded
atop a stump

when they died
she pulled them whole
    into the dump back there
too old to dig a hole
    for her nanny goats
no help around

rumor has it
she's back there too
    covered up
all the hazel branches
    arching
    weighted with nuts
    rough skins
    hard shell

I don't go back there.

iii
Walking by me nary a nod
the clogged lady has a shovel
as if she gets free range
      of our private place
      of killed things
as if she'll find
      what she needs there

he says *She's an artist*
      takes stuff
      shells driftwood gewgaws
      hearts carved in mushrooms
      a little seagull sitting on a spike
      stuck into the wood
she glues them into a box
folks open the lid
look in
      all this in a box

Jack off in a box I say

That's not funny he says.

iv

I watch him watch the artist lady
   from nowhere return
her mouth fresh with red lipstick

she steps aside to get past me
she shows him her finds
   our losses
     wishbone jawbones joints skull
     skins hard-tanned with cedar seep

who is he to her
a salty man in generous pants
   its zipper ends at his belt
   where his fly shuts
   with a safety pin
he loves that belt
   gotten some place in Idaho
someplace close
to where he was a kid.

Wife—
Piano Tuner

i
The Kraut let the boys
pry off the hood ornament
    three-pointed star in a circle
    flashy hubcaps
    bug-eyed headlamps
Mercedes-Benz royal blue
    came with him
    as the war took off
the boys like crows working
    on something shiny
    enemy foreign

the boys boxed his ears
the old German this piano tuner
    lost his hearing

he drives by for me
    my feet on his stuff
    saved from vandals
the toolbox
    tuning forks hammer
    wedges mutes
he keeps next to his thigh
    his side of the shift

my true love stays
in the cabin not getting up
to delay our going
with questions.

ii

He lays out his tools
    in the music room
next to the Queen Victoria
    her knobbed legs powerful
    rounded Cape Horn
    lashed and padded securely
    below deck
    priceless

above us
a sepia photo
    thirteen sons and daughters pose
    all pale all buttons all ironed goods
gather behind parents
    in straight back chairs
    boys in the back row
    girls with stilled hands lovely
gone to Seattle and a house of stone
their grand piano stayed

always the rumor
they'd be back
    not for the piano
but for the Fourth of July
    war over
    younger sons home.

iii

I come to hear for him
humidity rises
 between the ocean
 and rain forest
the soundboard swells
 strings stretched
 pitch sharpened
he tightens the tuning pins
he presses a key
taps the fork
the two vibrate
pair like lovely ladies
 in double lines dancing
 across the blond floor

the notes jangle
the dancers trip
I slap the piano
he feels the tremor
 of my disapproval

years now empty house
 walls floors giving over
he dusts and oils
the grand piano
 the queen's rosewood
 bone and ebony keys
 timber money
I don't ask if he is paid.

44

iv

As he repacks
I take the bench
   raise my hands
   curl my fingers
   set my soul
for my recital piece
never played again
after my big brother
turned to drift at Dunkirk

for years
I had no piano
   no music
   sharp or flat
   ascending and descending
   high or low

I play Listz
   Harmonies du Soir
its notes mob the chords
   treble a golden glaze
   all fingers and crossing hands
then out of the frenzy
single note after note
they too cease
and one more note vibrates
spends itself along the wire

               *

exits the piano body
    stretching running
    resonance ribboning
    in a long exhale
then thick silence spans
    what note next what note next
    aching for that note
will it be when will it be
I hit the note
    its vibration
    a stretch of ecstasy.

v

I get home
my true love sits by the stove
    not stoking his perfect fire
    not coming to bed to me
morning he is better
    makes coffee
    pours blackstrap
    molasses into his oats
his spoon hits the bowl
discordant tat tat tat tat tat
running together crowded.

Husband—
Turning

I'll be drunk before
the sun sets
chasing sleep
before the sun rises

the moon climbs
    the night window
the radio finds
    its white voice
    spanning the hours

soon dawn
stands in the yard
I walk into it
    fence grass bench
everything is equal
without shadow yet

time tightens
    not so exactly
I step and turn

home was never here.

Wife—
Treefrogs

i
John Tornow
    he's out there yet
Wild Man of the Wynoochee
he tethers treefrogs
    to sticks with threads
unraveled from his cuffs
    frayed from months
    alone bushwhacking

he sleeps
    the frogs' aria
    covering him
until quiet startles him awake
to trouble stalking the trail
    deputies noisy with packs
    clicking and pistols cocking.

ii
Inside here
at the big table
my love says
I'm going east
    over the mountains
    Yakima snow clear

February dawn
his bingeing
    no longer
    breaks the night
    smothering us

I say
Please stay
row me out
    on the pond
on your raft
    topsy-turvy
    careful
    make-do

I say
John Tornow
is on the loose
stay

he says
Tornow's dead
years now

I say
No matter
he's out there
stay

he says
It's you
not him.

iii
Alone
midnight
the full moon shines
    off the rimed grass
    light scattering
    like shattered glass
my opening the door
shuts down
the frog noise
as if I'm not welcome
out where I pick it clean
    salal ferns foxglove
and strip bark
    chittum and cedar
and dig
    ginger and camas

if I could
I'd knot my nerves
    stiff as waxed string
into a net and cast
    filling it with dark
    and mute frogs

from the willows
John Tornow
watching me

I leave the door open
climb back into bed
warming

frog chorus
floods the house.

iv

Dawn
my love is home
    driven all night
hands frozen tight
    around dollars earned
winter-pruning orchards

I clean his boots
    of apple slurry
capped by an icy crust
last autumn's fruit fall
    fermented
red-shafted flickers
    drunk on it

I say *Sleep never came*
I open his fist
pry out the night
replace it
    with a moth's flutter

John Tornow tunnels
    into the hardhack
    his wild self
    panicked at being seen.

Husband—
Bunking Next To The Dead

The beach grows
where the current lags
sand falling
    from the slowing drift

I don't read the dates
    on the pioneer gravestones
    near where I bed down

    heavy with song
white-crowned sparrows
    fill the night
    to empty themselves

the dead cross over
    one by one to try the latch
    soft loud all the night

the knife is missing
its bone-handled blade
honed keen as a loon's cry.

Wife—
Forest Fire

i
The school bus comes
we all get on
    kids moms dads loners
    and the slowly dying
we who have houses
but no money no supplies
    hand to mouthers
    water system out
    kerosene and woodstove
    in this rainless September

we disembark
    behind the bakery
    descend the deep stairs
to line up
    at the Red Cross canteen

we take what we can get
he says *Never too much*
    catsup and sugar packs
we share a shower
almost hot.

ii

We walk through
    what's left of town
not flames
but a loaded downdraft
    blinking with embers
split at the hill's back side
its heat forced through
the two gaps north of town
    converging sparking
    here and there
to pick its prey

a townie displays mugs
    pulled out of the kiln
    that was her house
She says *Take one*
    she sits on a stuffed sofa
    rescued by her sons

my love rubs a crinkled mug
he says *Still some use*
I say *Leave it*
they look at me
    like I'm Herod
    sacrificing Baby Jesus
I don't like him
    finding value
    in a cracked cup.

Wife—
Bets

Up the creek
    through char and ash
we play find the place

fire hopscotched
    through the fir tops
some trunks all black

he says *The driveway*
and her cabin there still
    no windows broken

I say *Picky fire*

bear prints in the dust
    head to the creek

I say *She has to move*
    back now

He says *She won't.*

Wife—
Reconciliation

Glacier Motel
    gutters flush with rain
I wipe steam from the windows
he fiddles with the woodstove
    sputtering as the wind reverses
    like a liar found out

we take a walk for air
rising water erases
    the pond's edge
    flooding silver
    over the fields
silencing reed talk
and our talk

we hike up trail
    into the sun
among blueberries fermenting
    in autumn's last heat
kestrels walk sated

on the way back
we are more settled
grasshoppers descend

*

males riding females
scattering down the scree
at the trail's muddy edge
cougar tracks.

Husband—
Tsunami

They say
someday the sea
will pull back and the fish
will drown in air before the wave
returns

roaring
with God's vengeance
the wave transports inland
beached boats bull kelp logs and roofs mixed
with sea

people
dogs and chickens
lifted to ride the sea
soon pooling slacking pulling back
ripping

strong men
hug rooted trees
women children and chairs
ride out to sea and another
tall wave

swollen
with dying whales
and all the small Jonahs
the weaker Ahabs and us lost
at sea.

**Wife—
Shelling**

Distinctly
sun thin garden
I remember

peas in a pod
my dad's garden
I crack the pod
one pea imperfect
a green worm
    pokes out its head
    black pin-pricks for eyes

the pea is tastier
    given the bad worm
life is swell
what I've come to know
free peas grow from a seed
my mom said *No good*
wormy

I remember
my dad's climbing roses
    yellow orange like skirts
    of cha-cha dancers
    swirling lots of clacking
my mom said *They go wonky*
    roses blossoming untidily

my dad cut a start
stuck its wounded end
    into a potato
his mother did that
    coming west
this very rose
    climbing my fence
petals flat to the sun
    insides sticky
bumble bees hot at the pollen
bug and flower free for all.

Husband—
Wall

i
When the wind blows
something in the house shifts
something meaner
    than an earthquake
I escape through the back door
sun wavers through the firs
cold is visible
sun wakes the frozen dirt
fog forms
    eddies through me
    walking down to the wall

the garter snake
    is out
    its coil quickens
a frog traverses
    the rubble
the green thing
    becomes a bump inside
    the snake's progress

a crow drops for the snake
the crow's feathers turn white
no snake or frog or pale crow
stands a chance.

ii

She comes out on the porch
raises my rifle
    for one shot
    at the cursed crow
she never considers
I might step sideways
or cringe at the memory
    of blood spraying
    across the snow
American saviors
    retreating
    from St. Vith
boots full of slush

after the shot
I don't turn

God damn
she says
God damn.

Wife—
Damon Point

i
All day I am out
walking while there is sky

a hawk
de-winging a songbird
an elephant seal rolling
his bulk in the swash
a scarred bottle
    but no message
    Save me
my love is up beach
    in his pickup
    stop and go
headed this way
    beach wood

Yes I am here I am here
snowy owl spotted
    on a bleached log
    north back-dune
this year a Christmas maybe
dogs worry the owl
the bird rotates its head.

ii

I stand ankle deep in water
rain sheets across the sand
the flow uncovers
a grounded ship
I stand on her gunwale
    the topside salvaged
damp wicks up my pant legs

I am not alone
a beachcomber meanders
    the wrack line
straightens his walk toward me
    suspended in this expanse
    of light oaring west
dusk covers the dunes
like sleep over a naked body

Did you find anything I ask
    the man getting too close
he doesn't answer

against the rain I say
You're standing on a shipwreck

he asks *Where are you staying*

I say *I must get back to my husband*
I gesture to the road.

iii
At my car assorted guys
stand next to their tired truck
they are busy smoking weed

I am invisible
to be invisible
is an opened gift.

Husband—
Holly Wreath

i
She asks me again
Check up on him... her brother
    docked at the tribal marina
she never sends anything
no banana bread or jar of plums
she says *I've heard stuff*
    ask him if he's ready
    to bunk with us

The boat's her family gillnetter
cabin tricked out
    stove for heat
    water tank strapped to its back
she worked that boat in Alaska
    fishing with her dad
    and three brothers
    one washed overboard
she noticed and this brother didn't
    down below sleeping

he hasn't worked since the war
    Eleanor Roosevelt and Eisenhower
    send checks
               *

70

maybe for groceries
maybe for marina costs maybe not
tribes appreciate vets and guys so old
no one recalls if they are Indian
married Indian or just white
by happenstance
no one questions
a content albatross
that lands on your harbor.

ii

I sit on the dock
    first coffee then a flask
    drained to its low mark
his boat rides high today
    chimney smoking
he walks up the dock
old fart nods at me
pushes that handcart
    compliments of the marina
    garbage out
    groceries back

I throw a cigarette butt at him
he snags it
    end glowing
    measures the drags left
he tosses it into the water
seagulls rumple their wings
    then settle knowing how
    a cigarette flies
    how it lands how it pauses
    before sinking

he's wearing all he owns
    jeans t-shirt watch-cap slicker
his skin tanned to fruit leather
    squint lines cracking his face
his sister's lean look
    both of them starving
    in a world of plenty.

iii

I say *Let's have a drink*
I shake my flask at him

He says *I don't drink*
    too much bullshit
coming back drunk
    never make the jump
    from the dock to my deck
get dunked
my boat gumming me
    against the barnacles
I'm getting old.

74

iv

I say *She wants you*
to come live with us
    his sister by the door
    me by the woodstove
    just enough cash digging
    clams and picking greens
    cabin in the woods
    reeking outhouse cougars bears
    sugar ants in every bite

he says *She gave up*
the sea not me
the clinic says
I got 'til Christmas max
I'll die on the water
crossing the bar
    low tide high wind
    wave crests breaking
    big sea shallowing
come back then

the town women
    will launch
    a holly wreath
    at my empty slip.

v

Off he goes
    lucky sucker
I finish what's left
booze firing my belly
at least I got a woman
    no stranger ladies
    no do-gooders
    to send me off
and I try
my orchard bears apples
no matter the voles
    beneath and deer above
and wild fruit swelling
    on every sticker bush.

Wife—
Visiting

On the kitchen table
sake warm in a tin cup
with an opium chaser brewed
from her garden's poppies
fluttering black hearts
    pods milked green
she asks me to deflate
    the rising bread dough

she returns all favors
a twig with glowy lichen
    bumping its wet bark
a long-borrowed book
oysters breaded and fried
    in a lake of good butter

she returns my lost coat
its buttons tightened
heavier thread smarter knot
an almost-matching button
    replaces the lost one
in-and-out stitches
    making a cross

filling the window
her garden twists
into a gentle mass
vines kneel
    scarlet runner beans
abandoning the string
fraying
on the straight-up rows

she says
I can do nothing else for you.

Husband—
Sadiron

i
Just a boy
    ran from school
    go west young man
captain takes me on
    bastard

I jump ship
    off the stern
    into the flat sea
the next swell
    mounts
    high and forward
its wave cresting
    disassembling
    tumbling me
    withdrawing

one hundred dollars on my head
and the captain's pistol cocked

I work the beach
razor clams in burlap sacks
    drug along the sand

             *

resort to resort
I am gritty behind the ears
and no way to shower

girls smile at me
girls in white skirts pressed
    crisp by mothers lifting sadirons
    glowing hot off the woodstove.

ii
The seventh wave
spins a juvenile ratfish
    dying in the sea wrack
body gold dusted circus spotted
    blunt face
    empty eye sockets
    pectoral fins spread large
    like dragon wings

not shark not fish
some bones hard, some cartilage
a chimera

kids toe it
pull on its fleshy tags
    hanging from its belly
    like mistletoe
appendages for grasping
a mate's body
    for their flight spiraling
    into the blackening sea.

iii
A gyre of refuse
rides the Columbia's current
its leading edge
a flotilla of light bulbs

intact 40-watt screw-ins
    fresh not corroded
I collect six
    just in case

she's a widow now
I drank myself to death
my wake at the Green Lantern

her sea goes all
the way to Japan
where big waves
jolt into life
swell and roll east
toward the incandescent
    glow
    dim
    her bed lamp.

Wife—
South Of The Hoh

So wrong about death
I now eat black
crows eat what's left

I see him maybe
coming through the hemlock
I hear death's footfall

I see the earth curve
at the news of his death
rain climbs from the sea

I lower my arms
and raise them inhale death
green floods from the trees

no one told me
death arrives no one
told me rock erodes water

can I call the sun back
can I undo his death
sorrow steals my breath

what did I know
moths excite the day
snakes slide across night

it's all all death
I find ice in salt's sweet
and inhale windless breath.

Acknowledgments

Thank you, my poetry cohorts: Robert McNamara, Arlene Naganawa, John Davis, John Willson, Michael Spence, Sharon Hashimoto, Susan Landgraf, Sati Mookherjee.

The Vashon Haiku gathering and the Folio Poets Society at Seattle Athenaeum, Pike Place Market.

The residencies at Whiteley Center, Hedgebrook, and Espy.

Poet Adelaide Crapsey for her cinquain poem form.

The experts in specific worlds: plantsman John Browne, sailors Kaj Wyn Berry and David Steel, choker-setter and gillnetter James Addison Smith, musicologist Michael Tracy, and pianist Mark Salman playing Franz Liszt.

The local writers, including Edwin Van Syckle (*They Tried to Cut It All*), Ralph Andrews (*This Was Logging!*), Clara Weatherwax (*Marching! Marching!*), and Kurt Cobain (Nirvana everything).

The beach folks who greet me, the cafés who serve me breakfast. My grandparents for making a living on the beach and water, in the woods and schools along the Washington coast.

Ann Spiers is the inaugural Poet Laureate of Vashon Island in Washington State. She served as Vashon-Maury Audubon president and Land Trust staff, co-wrote *Walks, Trails and Parks on Vashon Island,* and stewards the Vashon Poetry Post.

Her poems appear widely in print and on-line in journals and anthologies. Her chapbooks include *What Rain Does* (Egress Studio), *Bunker Trail* (Finishing Line Press), and *Long Climb into Grace* (FootHills Publishing). Many of her lyrics are collected as art books. Her fine-art chapbooks—*The Herodotus Poems* (Brooding Heron Press) and *Volcano Blue, Tide Turn, A Wild Taste* (May Day Press)—are in private collections and the special collections at Stanford University, the University of Washington's Suzzallo Library, The British Library, Portland, Oregon's Multnomah County Library, and other libraries.

She received her Master in English Literature and Creative Writing degree from the University of Washington. She leads workshops in developing poem cycles and the art of chapbooks.

Web Page: www.AnnSpiers.com.